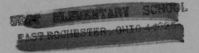

TEXAS

TEXAS

BETTY LOU PHILLIPS
AND BRYCE PHILLIPS

Franklin Watts
New York/London/Toronto/Sydney/1987
A First Book

Cover photographs courtesy of Shostal.

Photographs courtesy of: Texas Tourist
Development Agency (TTDA): pp. 13, 15, 33,
52, 88; TTDA/Michael Murphy: pp. 17, 43, 84;
Texas Highway Department: pp. 18, 21, 49, 60,
62, 65, 69; San Antonio Convention & Visitors
Bureau: pp. 29, 35; American Museum of Natural
History: p. 30; New York Public Library Picture
Collection: p. 38; Library of Congress: pp. 39, 64;
TTDA/Richard Reynolds: pp. 46, 57, 75, 81, 82;
Fred A. Schell: p. 71; Greater Houston Convention
& Visitors Council: p. 78; Austin, Texas
Chamber of Commerce: p. 85.

Library of Congress Cataloging-in-Publication Data

Phillips, Betty Lou.
Texas.

(A First book)
Bibliography: p.
Includes index.
Summary: Describes the history, geography, economy,
and principal cities of Texas.
1. Texas—Juvenile literature. [1. Texas]
I. Phillips, Bryce. II. Title.
F386.3.P48   1987   976.4   87-6229
ISBN 0-531-10395-1

CONTENTS

Introduction
9

Chapter One
The Land
11

Chapter Two
Indian Days
23

Chapter Three
Flags Over Texas
28

Chapter Four
The Republic of Texas
48

Chapter Five
Texas Joins the Union
51

Chapter Six
Texas Leaves the Union
54

Chapter Seven
The Growth of
Agriculture
59

Chapter Eight
The Rise of Industry
68

Chapter Nine
Texas Cities
77

Chapter Ten
Texas Today
87

Important Dates
in Texas History
89

For Further Reading
92

Index
93

TEXAS

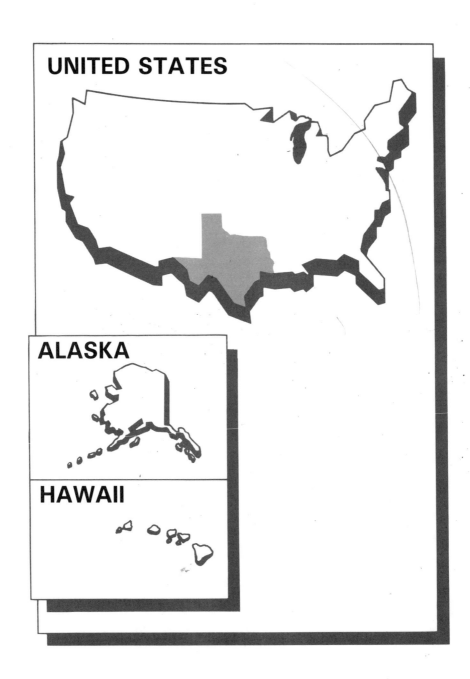

UNITED STATES

ALASKA

HAWAII

INTRODUCTION

Texas is the second largest state in the United States. It is as large as all of New England, New York, Pennsylvania, Ohio, and Illinois combined. It is more than 220 times the size of Rhode Island, the smallest state. Only Alaska is larger than Texas. But Texas has about thirty-five times as many people as Alaska; today more than 14 million people live in Texas.

The people and their dreams have given the state its character and made it great. They take pride in being Texans. What's more, Texans have never been shy about expressing their pride. They boast that the state capitol in Austin is seven feet higher than the nation's capitol in Washington, D.C. That men and women trained to take the first steps of the journey to the moon from the Lyndon B. Johnson Space Center near Houston, and that the trail to other planets begins there, too. That Texas has about sixty-two universities and colleges.

Houston is the nation's fourth largest city. The combined areas of Boston, Detroit, Atlanta, San Francisco, Denver, and Louisville could fit within its city limits. Houston is also the home of the nation's first domed and air-conditioned sports stadium, the world-famous Astrodome.

Cowboys and Indians, Longhorns and oil wells, tall tales and brave deeds by heroic men and women—all have long been associated with Texas. But the Texan of today is more likely to work in aerospace, telecommunications, or medicine.

—9

This land of great natural treasures also has a rich cultural heritage. During the nineteenth century, Texas was a magnet for Americans, Europeans, and people of Asian and African descent who sought a better life or a fresh start. These people played important roles in Texas history and became the founders of twentieth-century Texas.

Texas is called the Lone Star State because of the single star on its flag. Throughout the years, Texans have lived under the flags of six different countries: Spain, France, Mexico, the Republic of Texas, the Confederate States of America, and the United States of America. Texas joined the United States in 1845, but it withdrew from the Union along with the other southern states that seceded in 1861. For this reason, Texans often think of their state as a southern state rather than as a southwestern one.

1

THE LAND

Texas is the largest of the southern states. It stretches 801 miles (1687 km) from north to south and is nearly as long from east to west. Hardly anyone ever talks about Texas without mentioning its size.

But the size of Texas is not the characteristic that sets it apart from other states. It is the *land* that has created the jobs and built the fortunes in oil, cotton, cattle, and timber.

TERRAIN

In Texas, four great North American land masses meet. These are the Coastal Plains, the North Central Plains, the Great Plains, and the Mountains and Basins region. Although all are plains, each is different from the others in soil, topography, and vegetation. Each is also different beneath its surface.

In the eastern and southern areas of Texas, the rolling *Coastal Plains* span an area 100 to 300 miles (160 to 560 km) wide; they rise from sea level to about 700 feet (210 m). In the southern part of the Coastal Plains is the fertile lower Rio Grande River Valley. This valley is famous for its winter fruits and vegetables. From it, farmers ship Texas grapefruit, oranges, lemons, and limes to markets all over the country. Large crops of potatoes, tomatoes, canteloupes, and watermelons are also grown in this region. The sandy soil is excellent for farming, fruit growing, and cattle grazing.

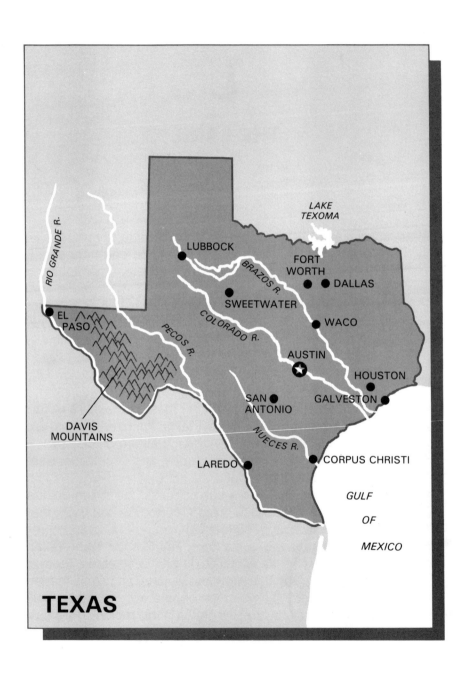

RIO GRANDE R.

LAKE
TEXOMA

LUBBOCK

FORT
WORTH

DALLAS

BRAZOS R.

SWEETWATER

WACO

EL
PASO

COLORADO R.

PECOS R.

AUSTIN

HOUSTON

DAVIS
MOUNTAINS

SAN
ANTONIO

GALVESTON

NUECES R.

LAREDO

CORPUS CHRISTI

GULF

OF

MEXICO

TEXAS

Preserved in its natural state, vast South Padre Island lies along the Texas coast.

Vast deposits of coal, gas, petroleum, salt, and sulfur lie under the soil of the Coastal Plains. The East Texas oil field was once one of the largest oil fields in the world.

Thick forests cover millions of acres in the Coastal Plains. Most of the trees are pine and cypress, but oak, pecan, and gum trees are also plentiful. More than 225 kinds of trees grow in Texas and more than 500 kinds of grasses.

The *North Central Plains* lie just to the west of the Coastal Plains. They rise in elevation from 750 feet (229 m) in the east to 2,500 feet (762 m) in the west. The western edge of this area is often called the Hill Country because of its rolling hills and valleys.

Some of the best farmland in Texas is located there. The rich, deep soils of the Black and Grand prairies produce sizable crops of cotton and grain. The grasslands are valuable livestock-grazing areas. The region is also an important producer of oil and gas.

The *Great Plains* reach westward from the North Central Plains into New Mexico, with sprawling stretches of high, flat plateaus. This land is 4,000 feet (1,219 m) high in the northwest. It slopes southward and down to 700 feet (213 m) above sea level. Cattle, goats, and sheep feed on the scraggly mesquite shrubs and grasses that cover the plateaus. There is little rainfall, and few large trees grow in this area.

The Texas Panhandle makes up a large part of the Great Plains area. It is the section in the northwestern part of the state that juts north and resembles the handle of a pan. The Panhandle produces more wheat than any other region of Texas. Ninety-five percent of the world's helium also lies in this area, as well as one of the richest petroleum and natural gas fields. Other mineral wealth includes building stones and salt.

The part of the Great Plains that lies along the border of Texas and New Mexico is called the High Plains. At first, settlers shunned this area because it is extremely dry. But in the late 1800s windmills were built to bring water to the surface of the arid land. Later, irrigation and dry-farming methods made the High Plains an important farming region.

—14

The scenery in Texas is breathtaking.

The *Mountains and Basins region,* in the westernmost part of the state, is the highest land in Texas. Its rocky, dry plains are crossed by spurs or extensions of the Rocky Mountains. Its tallest peak is Guadalupe Mountain, which rises 8,751 feet (2,670 m) above sea level.

It is also the sunniest and driest area of the state. Its flat land is mainly used for ranching. Ranchers rely on windmills for pumping water into ponds and tanks for their cattle. The Rio Grande also waters their crops.

STREAMS, RIVERS, AND LAKES

More than 3,700 Texas streams flow for 80,000 Texas miles. Many of them are navigable by canoe. At least thirty-nine of them are named Cottonwood Creek.

The largest river in the state is the winding Rio Grande. It forms the entire southern boundary of Texas, flowing 889 miles (1,431 km) through varying terrain, then emptying into the Gulf of Mexico. The swift current of the Rio Grande has worn deep channels with vertical walls in the mountainous Big Bend region. These canyons are already 2,000 feet (609 m) deep, and the Rio Grande keeps on cutting.

Texas has thousands of man-made lakes and ponds. One of the largest man-made lakes is Lake Texoma, a popular resort for fishing and boating. It covers 91,200 acres (36,480 hectares)— some of which lie in Oklahoma. Over the years, many of these lakes were built as a result of the state's various programs for generating electric power, irrigating farmlands, and storing water.

NATURAL RESOURCES

Texas is the nation's leading energy-producing state. It is rich in minerals, especially oil and natural gas. Billions of barrels of oil once lay beneath the plains. Texas produces millions of barrels of

*The mighty Rio Grande forms
the entire southern boundary of Texas.*

Oil refineries make gasoline
and other products from oil.

crude oil annually, or one-fourth of the nation's supply. One of the largest known natural gas reservoirs is in the Panhandle.

It is estimated that there are more than fourteen thousand uses for salt. Texas is an important producer of it. Underground salt veins occur in the Coastal Plains. Both underground and surface deposits have been found in West Texas. Surface deposits also appear in South Texas.

Valuable deposits of sulfur have been found in the Mountains and Basins region and in the Coastal Plains. Coal deposits cover about seventy-five thousand square Texas miles (194,250 sq km) from Laredo to Texarkana. Iron ore is found in the northeast. Texas also has a belt of limestone, gypsum, gravel, and silica sand.

PLANTS

Wildflowers grow almost everywhere in Texas—in woods, in fields, and in deserts; on prairies, along roadsides, and on hillsides; along streams and riverbanks. No place but Texas has more than five thousand species of native wildflowers. The bluish-purple bluebonnet is the state flower.

The wildflower show usually starts in early March and ends about six weeks later. To the amazement of many botanists, the flowers reseed themselves year after year. The Texas Highway Department helps out by scattering 71,000 miles (119,200 km) of seeds yearly. Flowers not only beautify the land; they also help keep soil from washing into ravines.

The National Wildflower Research Center, founded by Lady Bird Johnson on 60 acres (24 hectares) of land near Austin, encourages the use of native wildflowers, plants, trees, and shrubs in the landscaping plans of the country.

WILDLIFE

Texas is known for its wildlife. The state boasts 142 different native animal species. Mexican mule or black-tailed deer roam the Pecos

—19

River and Big Bend regions. Bighorn sheep, giant jackrabbits, coyotes, bobcats, ocelots, and wild hogs are found in various corners of Texas. The gray desert fox lives in the rocky, brush-covered country. And the small, harmless armadillo with its ridged armor shell can be spotted grazing almost anywhere.

The nation's largest herd of white-tail deer lives in Texas. Through game management programs, Texas has more deer now (over 4 million) than it did 150 years ago. White-tail deer are most numerous in South Texas and in the central parts of the state.

In Texas, the call to the hunt has always been strong. Hunting pumps millions of dollars annually into the state's economy and into the hands of ranchers who lease their lands to hunters and fishermen. Quail, dove, wild turkey, ducks, and geese are the chief game birds.

Brazosport, a community of nine cities, is the wild-bird capital of the nation. Ninety-seven percent of all known types of United States wild birds make their temporary homes during the winter on its sunny beaches. In the spring, flocks of birds sweep across Texas from the tropics on their way to their summer breeding grounds up north.

The mockingbird, famous for its ability to imitate the whistles and noises of other birds, was declared the official state bird in 1927. Today it is unlawful in Texas to kill or capture the feisty little copycat.

More cases of snakebite are reported annually in Texas than in any other state. About a hundred kinds of snakes live there. Most dangerous to people are the poisonous copperheads, rattlesnakes, cottonmouths, and Texas coral snakes. Each spring, Sweetwater hosts the world's largest rattlesnake round-up. At the twenty-eighth annual roundup in 1986, more than fifteen tons of rattlesnakes were captured. The longest was nearly six feet long.

Many kinds of fish live in Texas waters. Bass, catfish, and sunfish are abundant in fresh-water lakes. Brook and rainbow trout live in the rivers. Crabs, menhaden, oysters, and shrimp are found in the Gulf of Mexico.

—20

The armadillo, one of the state's more
unusual residents, was named by early Spanish
explorers, and means "the small armored one."

CLIMATE

Texas summers are hot. In the winter, however, the climate varies throughout the state. It can be freezing in North Texas and hot in South Texas at the same time. Generally, the farther north you are, the colder the winter weather is. But the weather in Texas can change suddenly. A fast-moving cold front called a "norther" can whistle through the Panhandle and Central Texas and lower temperatures 40 degrees Fahrenheit (15° C.) in a few hours.

Sleet from the north may ice most of the state in the winter, but snow seldom falls in the central regions. The heaviest snowfalls occur in the High Plains, where about twenty-four inches of snow fall annually. The coldest area is the Panhandle. The warmest area is the lower Rio Grande Valley. There January temperatures average 60 degrees Fahrenheit (16° C.). El Paso, in far West Texas, has more sunny days than any other U.S. city.

Rainfall in the state decreases from east to west. During the spring, brief thunderstorms with heavy rains and gusty winds batter Central Texas. Strong winds create dreadful duststorms in West Texas. About a hundred tornadoes touch down each year, more than in any other state. Since 1950, Houston's Harris County has reported more tornadoes than any other county in the entire United States.

During the summer and fall, high winds and heavy rains sometimes join the waters of the Gulf of Mexico to pound the Texas coast. These violent storms are *hurricanes.* Like sledgehammers, they can cause widespread destruction to the cities, towns, and people in their paths. When a hurricane focused its anger on Galveston Island on September 8, 1900, more than six thousand Texans were killed. Most of them drowned when water flooded the city. A second powerful hurricane hit Galveston in 1915 and claimed 275 lives, but a new seawall saved the city from destruction.

In 1983, Hurricane Alicia struck the Texas coast. It was the most costly hurricane in history.

INDIAN DAYS

For hundreds of years Indians were the only people who lived in what is now Texas. When white explorers first came to Texas, about thirty thousand Indians made their homes there. They lived in scattered groups called tribes. In many ways Texas Indians were alike, but in some ways, the various tribes differed.

Each tribe had its own laws, customs, folk tales, and dances. Each tribe also had its own way of worshipping the gods it believed in. Because the tribes lived in different climates, they had assorted building materials available to them, so they built different kinds of homes. Villages usually sprouted along riverbanks, where the land was fertile and easily tilled.

Texas Indian tribes spoke many different languages. They also developed a sign language, using their hands and fingers to express what they wanted to say. Without an alphabet, the Indians could not keep records or write down their thoughts and feelings. Instead, they painted pictographs, or word pictures, on cave walls, rocks, and hides. Sometimes they carved petroglyphs on rock or clay, using sharp tools. These drawings can be found on the walls of caves and on the sides of cliffs throughout Texas.

THE FARMERS

The Caddo Indians built their villages in the Piney Woods of East Texas, near the Louisiana border. The Wichita tribe settled along the Red River, near the area now called Dallas and Fort Worth. Both the Caddoes and the Wichitas dwelled in dome-shaped grass huts that looked like tall beehives. Usually two families lived together in one large, enclosed hut. Each family also had a smaller hut with open sides for resting, working, and storing food.

The Caddoes and Wichitas were mainly farmers. Both men and women worked hard clearing fields and planting and caring for crops. Often the men trapped rabbits, coyotes, beavers, and foxes and hunted javelina (a relative of the wild boar) and bear. During the summer, they hunted bison, or buffalo, on the plains where the great herds gathered. Before horses and guns were brought to Texas, the Indians killed the herds by stampeding them over cliffs. Then they pulled each bulky animal home on a travois, a V-shaped sled made of saplings. A grown bull weighed between 1,600 and 2,600 pounds.

The farming Indians ate the buffalo meat and used the hides for bedcovers, robes, and moccasin soles. Buffalo and deerskin clothes were made by the women of the tribe. They also molded clay pots and jugs for cooking and drinking. Most historians believe the Caddo and Wichita Indians were the most advanced Indians living in Texas.

Although some men chose to be warriors, these tribes were mainly peace-loving people. All painted their bodies with bright colors and wore shells, bones, and animal teeth around their necks. Both men and women hung ornaments from their pierced ears. Caddo men also hung decorations from their noses; the name *Caddo* means "pierced nose."

Like all Texas Indians, the Caddoes and Wichitas practiced tattooing. Using sharp rocks or thorns, men and women scratched stripes and circles onto their faces and drew birds and plants on their bodies. Then they rubbed ashes into the scratches so that blue scars remained when the skin healed.

Most farming tribes held planting ceremonies, rain dances, and harvest festivals. But for the Jumano Indians, farming was a difficult task. They lived along the Rio Grande in West Texas, where there

—24

was little rainfall. Since they did not know how to irrigate the land, their crops often withered and died, and families often starved.

Jumanos lived in square houses called pueblos. These were made of stone or adobe, a mixture of ash, dry grass, mud, and water that hardens in the sun.

THE FISHING PEOPLES

Bands of Karankawa Indians lived along the Gulf Coast between what is now Galveston and Corpus Christi. The Atakapans settled to the north, near the lower Trinity and San Jacinto rivers. Fishing tribes seldom stayed more than a week in one spot; they camped in brush shelters and roamed the coastal waters in search of food. Among their favorites were oysters, clams, scallops, and turtles. The fishing Indians also hunted alligators in creeks; then they smeared their bodies with melted alligator grease and mud to keep away mosquitoes in the bays and swamps.

These Indians moved around in canoes. Their canoes were made of tree trunks cut in two and hollowed out by scraping and burning. Most canoes were long enough to hold an entire family and all its possessions.

The Atakapan people were short and stout. In contrast, the Karankawa were tall and strong. They wore pieces of cane in holes cut through their lower lips and chests. One Karankawa custom forbade a brave, once he married, to speak to his wife's parents or to set foot in their home ever again.

All fishing Indians believed that a pointed head was a mark of beauty. To shape it, they tied a thin board padded with moss to each baby's head for a year.

THE PLANT GATHERERS

The Tonkawas lived along the rivers and creeks of Central Texas, while the Coahuiltecans made their homes inland from what is now Galveston to the Rio Grande and eastward toward San Antonio.

—25

Like the fishing Indians, the Tonkawas and Coahuiltecans spent most of the year searching for food; they, too, camped in brush shelters along streams.

But these tribes also gathered pecans, acorns, and mesquite beans. They liked sunflower seeds, herbs, roots, and fruits as well. The fruit of the prickly-pear cactus was their favorite. When food was scarce, they sometimes ate worms, spiders, and lizards. Buffalo were rare in this region. Instead, the Indians hunted deer, antelope, rabbits, turtles, snakes, and javelinas.

The Tonkawas frequently traded flint with other tribes for needed food and supplies. Flint was used for making arrowheads and spears. For centuries, the bow and arrow was the Indians most useful weapon.

It was customary for Coahuiltecans to mourn for three months male relatives who died. During this time mourners could not leave camp, even in search of food. Because they depended upon others, grieving Coahuiltecans often starved.

THE HUNTERS

The Indians of West Texas were hunters. They were also fierce warriors who struggled constantly for control of the plains. Bands of Comanches, Lipan Apaches, and Kiowas roamed from the Panhandle to the Rio Grande and into Mexico and New Mexico. As they fought over the best hunting grounds, they camped along streams in cone-shaped teepees made of buffalo hides that had been sewn together and painted with designs.

The hunting tribes lived on buffalo. They ate the meat, used the hides for clothing and teepees, and made tools and spoons from the bones and horns.

Because the hunting tribes liked to kill, they were the most feared and hated Indians in Texas. They considered everyone their enemy, and they fought with and stole from all. When Spanish settlers arrived in Texas in the early 1600s, the Indians stole from them, too.

The Comanches robbed the settlers of their horses, became fine horsemen, and followed the buffalo wherever they went. On horseback, the Comanches could also raid other tribes and escape before being attacked. As a result, they were the most dreaded of all tribes. The farming tribes were no match for the Comanches, nor were the fishing people or the plant gatherers. All ended up fighting each other as well as the white man—whom they tried to keep out of Texas.

3

FLAGS OVER TEXAS

When Christopher Columbus arrived in the Americas in 1492, he claimed the New World for Spain. In 1519, the Spanish governor of Jamaica sent Alonso Alvarez de Piñeda to explore the shores of the Gulf Coast. As he sailed from Florida to Mexico, Captain Piñeda mapped the coastline. At the spot where the Rio Grande empties into the Gulf of Mexico, he stopped and repaired his ship. Most historians believe that Captain Piñeda was the first European in Texas. Before sailing on, he raised the flag of Spain over Texas. For the next three hundred years, Texas was owned by Spain.

THE SPANISH EXPLORERS

In 1528, a group of Spanish explorers on their way to Mexico were shipwrecked off Galveston Island. They were taken prisoner by the Karankawa Indians and were forced to search for food in the ocean bays and inlets of South and Central Texas. The Indians told them tales of gold and great wealth in large cities. Years later, the leader of the group, Alvar Nuñez Cabeza de Vaca, and three of his men escaped from their captors. They made their way to Mexico, where other Spaniards lived. In Mexico City, the men repeated the Indians' tales to the other Spaniards.

When Cabeza de Vaca returned to Spain, he wrote a book about his adventures. His stories made other men long to explore Texas.

—28

The Villa of San Fernando was made the capitol of the Spanish province of Texas. The Spanish governors resided in this "Governor's Palace," which bears a keystone dated 1749.

*This painting depicts Coronado starting on his
search for the Seven Cities of Cibola.*

The Spaniards sent many expeditions to look for the fabled golden cities, called the Seven Cities of Cibola.

In 1540, Francisco Vasquez de Coronado led one of these expeditions. He traveled from Mexico across the plains of West Texas as far north as the Panhandle. Instead of cities rich in gold, Captain Coronado found only Indian towns and villages. He returned to Mexico City empty-handed.

But his expedition was important. Not only did he claim more land for Spain, but he also had learned a great deal about the land, animals, plants, and Indians of Texas. In the Rocky Mountains, he discovered the Continental Divide. This is the place where North American waters separate: some waters drain westward into the Pacific Ocean, and others flow eastward into the Atlantic Ocean.

Captain Coronado didn't find the golden cities, and there was no further Spanish exploration for a long time. Then Spaniards began to explore Texas again. They made maps of rivers, plains, and mountains.

At first, some of the Indians were friendly and generous with their supplies. In fact, most Texans believe that the name Texas comes from the Indian word *tejas,* which means "friendly."

Soon there was trouble, however. Even the friendly Indians found that feeding extra people and animals was no easy task. What's more, the hunting tribes did not take kindly to the invasion of their territory or to white men killing buffalo grazing on the plains. The Indians raided, fought back, and killed.

To try to civilize the Indians, Spanish priests were sent into Texas to build missions, small farms around a church. The priests asked the Indians to live in the missions. To protect the missions, soldiers lived in nearby forts called presidios. The priests hoped to teach the Indians about the Christian god and how to be farmers and Spanish citizens.

But life in the missions was very different from the life the Indians had known. There was a set schedule. Each day began with religious studies. Afterward, the men were taught blacksmithing, carpentry, farming, and animal care. The women learned to weave.

—31

The first Spanish mission was built in 1682; it still stands today in Ysleta, near El Paso. Later, missions for the Indians were built all over Texas. The largest and most successful was Los Adaes, in present-day Louisiana. It was named the first capital of Spanish Texas in 1721.

THE FRENCH

The French, too, were interested in the Southwest. Robert Cavelier, Sieur de la Salle, traveled down the Mississippi River in 1682 and claimed the entire river valley for France. He named the region Louisiana in honor of the French king, Louis XIV. Cavelier led French settlers into Texas in 1685. They raised the French flag on Matagorda Bay and built Fort Saint Louis.

Although many of the French settlers were fine carpenters, few were farmers. When supplies ran low, they fought with each other over them. Sieur de la Salle was killed by one of his own men. Sickness and Indians killed the others. By 1689, only a weak French claim to Texas remained.

Nonetheless, in 1714 France sent Louis Saint Denis to make friends with the Texas Indians and to trade French goods for furs. The furs were sold in Canada and France for a handsome profit. Because Spanish leaders distrusted Saint Denis and disliked his influence over the Indians, they put him in jail. Then the French built their trading posts in Louisiana, across the Texas border.

Still, French settlers kept moving west into Texas. Fearing the French might push them out, Spanish leaders built more of their own settlements in Texas. They also sent an army of soldiers to protect the settlers—and to turn back the French.

THE FOUNDING OF
SAN ANTONIO

By 1718, travelers needed a South Texas stopping place between the Spanish settlements on the Rio Grande and those in East Texas.

One of the early missions at El Paso

As a result, the Spanish founded a new mission with high walls on the San Antonio River called San Antonio de Valero. Later it was called the Alamo, the Spanish word for the cottonwood trees that surrounded the mission.

The priests at the missions worked hard to teach the Indians to be craftsmen and farmers, but the Indians often held on to their ancient customs. The Indians preferred their own way of life and many returned to the wilderness. Mission after mission failed.

Then the Comanches began to push the Apaches deeper into South Texas. Apache raids on Spanish settlements, missions, and presidios became more frequent. Not surprisingly, the Spanish became less eager to build new settlements. After more than a hundred years of missions and over a hundred expeditions, there were still only about seven thousand European settlers in Texas.

France temporarily lost her claim to Louisiana in 1753. After that, Spanish leaders felt that France was no longer a threat in East Texas. There was no longer a need for costly missions or settlements there. So the Spanish forced five hundred settlers to leave their homes, crops, and much of their livestock and to move to San Antonio. The settlers were very unhappy about this. Worse still, some of their children died along the way. When they arrived, many families found that they disliked living in the Hill Country. In 1779, Gil Ibarvo led thirty of them back east. They settled in Nacogdoches, which later became one of the most important towns in Spanish

Mission San Francisco de la Espada was the first of five San Antonio missions to be built of stone and was established by Franciscan priests.

Texas. The large stone fort where the early settlers hid during Indian attacks is one of the oldest buildings in Texas.

UPRISING AGAINST SPAIN

By 1810, Spain was having trouble holding on to its New World empire, which included much of North America. After living under Spanish rule for nearly three hundred years, the Mexican people began to want to rule themselves. They had seen the Americans win their freedom from England in 1783. They also had watched the people of France rise up against their king. Now the desire for freedom from Spanish rule caused the Mexican people to revolt.

Those who wanted Texas to break away from both Mexico and Spain were called "filibusters." Filibusters Augustus Magee and Bernardo Gutiérrez led a small army and captured Nacogdoches and Goliad in 1812. They claimed that the settlers were then free from Spanish rule, but this was not so.

In 1821, Mexico won its independence from Spain. Since Texas was a province of Mexico, Mexico's flag now waved in place of Spain's. Texas became part of the Mexican state of Coahuila.

AMERICAN SETTLEMENTS

Like the earlier Spanish rulers, the new Mexican leaders did not welcome settlers to Texas from the United States. But starting in 1815, Anglo-Americans from Kentucky and Tennessee began settling in the northeastern part of Texas anyway. About eighty families were allowed to stay, only because no one was sure who owned that part of Texas after the Louisiana Purchase. Spanish Texas might have had only a few towns if banker Moses Austin had not changed the course of Texas history.

In 1820, Austin rode a mule all the way from Missouri to San Antonio to request permission to bring three hundred Anglo-American families to Texas. When he arrived, Governor de Martinez refused to see him. Austin then obtained the help of Baron de Bastrop, a European who was friendly with Spanish officials, and his request was approved. But Moses Austin didn't live to see his dream come true. His dying wish was that his son, Stephen, carry out his plan.

The first American colony in Texas was founded by Stephen Fuller Austin. He is known as the "Father of Texas."

TEXAS PIONEERS

Opportunity lured the adventurous west. Courageous men and women with a yearning for land of their own came to Texas to better their lives.

Since there were no stores in that part of Mexico in 1821, those who pioneered the first settlements packed food, water, cooking utensils, clothing, and seeds. Most also packed axes and saws for use in clearing frontier lands for farming.

Many people traveled from Nashville down the Natchez Trace to Natchez, where they boarded steamboats headed for New Orleans. Schooners then carried these pioneers to Galveston. Others struggled overland, at the rate of fifteen or twenty miles (24 or 32 km) a day, in heavy canvas-covered wagons pulled by oxen and mules.

The first U.S. colonies in Texas were founded in the fertile East Texas land along the lower Brazos and Colorado rivers. At Washington-on-the-Brazos and Columbus, settlers cut, sawed, and dragged logs to spots they chose for their homes.

Stephen Austin was a strong leader. He made peace with the Indians, wrote laws for his colonies, and helped the settlers plant their crops. Because of his hard work, the Mexican government gave him permission to bring five hundred more families to Texas. In 1823, San Felipe de Austin became the colony's seat of government. But the settlers still had to obey the laws of Mexico.

New land grants—at 100 to 120 dollars per family—opened the

Many brave men and women ventured west to Texas.

Stephen Austin, the "Father of Texas"

way for more Americans to settle in Texas. Of the twenty-six *im-presarios*—men authorized to sell land—who worked to bring settlers to Texas, Stephen Austin was the most successful.

Some new families brought slaves and built large cotton and rice plantations in Central and East Texas. A small number of free blacks—about one in ten—also found their way there. By 1830, nearly twenty-five thousand people lived in Texas. Most of them were from the United States.

TROUBLE IN TEXAS

In 1827 President John Quincy Adams offered Mexico a million dollars for Texas. Two years later, President Andrew Jackson raised the offer to 5 million. Although Mexican leaders rejected both offers, the United States' interest in Texas troubled Mexican leaders. They worried that the Americans would soon want Texas to become an independent state. Or worse yet, they might try to make Texas a part of the United States. As a result, a law was passed in 1830 forbidding Americans to move to Texas. But in spite of the law, thousands more settlers crossed the U. S. border.

Soon American settlers outnumbered the Mexicans. By 1833, colonists not only wanted more say in Texas lawmaking, they also wanted some of the present laws changed. They were not against belonging to Mexico, but they wanted Texas to be an independent state. Stephen Austin was asked to voice the wants of the people. He was sent to Mexico City to talk to the Mexican leaders.

In Mexico City, months passed before the leaders would see Austin. When they finally did, they promised him better laws for Texas. But Austin was thrown in jail. He was not told why he was arrested, nor was he brought to trial. For nearly a year, Mexican officials would not permit him to talk to anyone because they feared that he planned for Texas to break away from Mexican rule.

More than two years passed before Stephen Austin returned

home a free man. The colonists were happy to see him, but they were angry at Mexico.

THE TEXAS REVOLUTION

Meanwhile, a revolt had taken place in Mexico. In 1834 General Antonio Lopez de Santa Anna seized control of the Mexican government and became dictator. He did not believe in democracy, so he threw out the constitution that Mexico had adopted in 1824. Instead of granting more freedom to the people, as he had promised he would, he took away some of their rights. He refused to allow Texans to elect their own leaders. The Texas settlers paid little attention to these new Mexican laws, however.

Determined that everyone would obey him, Santa Anna sent soldiers to take away the settlers' guns and collect taxes. But guns were among the colonists' most important possessions. Without them, they could neither fight raiding Indians, nor shoot game for food. Angry Texans finally had had enough of Mexican rule. Rather than give up their rights, they would fight for freedom from Mexico.

A lawyer named Sam Houston, a new colonist leader, had come to Texas as an Indian agent. He had also been a soldier, U. S. Congressman, and governor of Tennessee. He wanted Texas to separate from Mexico—and to join the United States.

Led by Colonel William Travis, Texas rebels captured Fort Anahuac on June 30, 1835. Four months later, the Mexicans were driven from the town of Gonzales when they tried to take away the town's only cannon. At San Felipe de Austin, Texas leaders organized a temporary government. Then Colonel Ben Milam and the rebels marched west to San Antonio, the Mexican capital of Texas.

In early December, rebels from all over Texas surrounded San Antonio. They kept Mexican troops and supplies from entering or leaving the city while they stormed the presidio of San Antonio de Bexar and the Alamo. After four days, General Martin Perfecto de

Cos, Santa Anna's brother-in-law, who was defending the capital, surrendered.

Some of the rebels headed for Goliad after this victory. Others returned to their farms and ranches. About a hundred Texans remained at the Alamo. Colonel William Travis and twenty-six others joined them. A month later, thirty Mexicans sent to blow up the Alamo disregarded their orders and stayed. Now there were about 160 men at the Alamo.

When Santa Anna heard that the Mexican troops had surrendered at San Antonio, he was outraged. In the dead of winter, he ordered five thousand soldiers to march two thousand miles north from Mexico City to San Antonio. This time he commanded the army himself.

The arrival of Santa Anna's army took Texans in the Alamo by surprise. Colonel Travis sent his best friend, James Butler Bonham, to get help—and he hoped his men would be able to hold the old Spanish mission until it arrived. He offered each man a choice—either leave or stay and fight. Everyone knew that there was no way the Alamo could stand against Santa Anna's army. Yet all but one man stayed.

The Mexican soldiers surrounded the Alamo. Santa Anna demanded that the Texans surrender. But Colonel Travis bravely declared, "I shall never surrender or retreat!" Then a red flag rose over Santa Anna's post: now no one would be taken alive.

From Gonzales came about thirty more rebel fighters, but that was all. Still, the Texans—some of Mexican descent—refused to surrender the Alamo. The fiery siege began on February 23 and lasted eleven long days. Santa Anna's troops shelled the Alamo both day and night until rebel ammunition was so low the weary Texans could no longer return Mexican fire.

At dawn on March 6, Santa Anna's men rushed the fort. The Texans used their muskets as clubs and put up a fierce fight. But within the hour the Alamo fell, and all its defenders lay dead. Among

The Alamo. The thirteen-day siege there in 1836 is known as one of the most heroic struggles in history.

the brave men who gave their lives for Texas were the frontiersman Davy Crockett and Jim Bowie, the maker of the famous Bowie knife. In all, 187 men laid down their lives so that Texas might be independent from Mexico. Santa Anna spared the life of one woman, Mrs. Dickinson, so that she could spread the tale of the Alamo and frighten Texans into giving up their ideas of freedom.

A NEW GOVERNMENT FOR TEXAS

None of those fighting at the Alamo knew that Texan leaders had declared Texas's independence and had formed a new republic in an unfinished blacksmith's shop at Washington-on-the-Brazos. On March 2, 1836, fifty-nine delegates signed a Declaration of Independence stating that Texas was an independent nation and no longer part of Mexico. Like the Constitution of the United States, the Texas Constitution set up three branches of government—the executive, legislative, and judicial. The leaders named David G. Burnet as temporary president until the war ended. They named Sam Houston commander-in-chief of the army and sent Stephen Austin for help from the United States.

THE RUNWAY SCRAPE

After the fall of the Alamo, Texans met one defeat after another. As Santa Anna's men marched east from San Antonio, thousands of settlers fled, knowing they were no match for the oncoming Mexican army. People felt they were in a "scrape." They left their homes behind, and their flight became known as the Runaway Scrape.

In Gonzales, 374 volunteers awaited Sam Houston. None knew the Alamo had fallen. Also unaware was General Houston, until he was told by two Mexicans. To keep this news from spreading, he put the two men in jail. Then he sent his scout, Erastus "Deaf" Smith, to verify their story. On the way to San Antonio, "Deaf" Smith met Mrs. Dickinson, who said that Santa Anna had promised to kill every Texan who fought against his rule.

When word reached Gonzales, people panicked. Hurriedly, families gathered their belongings and poured out of town. The heavy spring rains flooded the roads, streams, and rivers. Some soldiers lent people helping hands, while others returned to their families.

Suddenly, the future of Texas depended on whether General Houston could gather enough men to battle Santa Anna and whether he could train his men to win over a much larger force. Only a few men accompanied General Houston out of Gonzales. But as he moved eastward, many men joined his army. News of the Alamo brought the people of Texas together in their fight against Mexico.

THE BATTLE OF SAN JACINTO

The general saw only one way to defeat Santa Anna: to make his army a match for the Mexican troops. Then he could choose the time and place for a surprise attack. But until he had enough men and supplies, he had to retreat.

For nearly six weeks, Santa Anna and 1,200 men stomped through East Texas hunting Sam Houston and his army. The Texans hid, while General Houston drilled his 910 men. Then two small cannons arrived from the people of Cincinnati, Ohio, who sympathized with the Texans' struggle for freedom.

From his scouts, General Houston learned that Santa Anna had crossed the Buffalo Bayou. At last Sam Houston saw his chance. With Santa Anna in front of him, he no longer retreated. Instead, he sought a place for a surprise attack.

On the afternoon of April 21, 1836, Houston's scouts reported that Mexican soldiers had been seen napping in a nearby meadow at San Jacinto. Boldly, Texas freedom fighters hauled their "twin sisters" cannons almost into the Mexican camp. Then they opened fire.

Shouting "Remember the Alamo!" and "Remember Goliad!", the angry Texans showed no mercy. In eighteen bloody minutes, the battle was won. Almost every man in the Mexican army was either killed or captured. Only nine Texans had died. Thirty were wounded, including General Houston, who was shot in the ankle.

But the war was not over. Santa Anna himself had managed to escape. If Santa Anna succeeded in reaching the main force of his army, no rebel army on Texas soil could beat him.

As it happened, General Houston's decision to burn Vince's Bridge led to Santa Anna's capture. The disguised Mexican dictator was caught eight miles from the battlefield near the ruins of the bridge, looking for a way to cross the bayou because he could not swim. To save his life, he agreed that Texas was free from Mexican rule. He also promised that nearby Mexican forces would retreat beyond the Rio Grande and not fight again.

Rising 570 feet over the flat coastal plain, the San Jacinto Monument commemorates the decisive defeat of Santa Anna's forces by Sam Houston's army of Texans in 1836. The landmark is located east of downtown Houston.

THE REPUBLIC
OF TEXAS

At last Texas was free. The Lone Star flag flew proudly over the new country—the Republic of Texas. In September 1836, the people elected their hero, General Sam Houston, president. He defeated the former head of the Texas government, Henry Smith, and Stephen Austin. The voters chose Mirabeau Lamar to be vice-president. Then Stephen Austin, Thomas Rusk, and Henry Smith were asked to help govern the new republic according to a constitution that guaranteed freedom.

In January 1837 the capital was moved to the new town of Houston. Many tasks faced those setting up the new government, including finding ways to pay for it. The republic started out being more than a million dollars in debt.

During his presidency, Sam Houston spent much time dealing with troubles between the Indians and settlers. He also started courts and a post office, divided Texas into counties, and laid out public lands. Today Texas has 254 counties—more than any other state.

In 1838, Texans elected Mirabeau Lamar the second president of the republic. President Lamar needed help from other nations in getting Mexico to recognize Texan independence and to stop threatening war. Without acceptance from other countries and open trade, Texas could not become a strong nation. At that time, however, only the United States accepted Texas as a free republic, so the

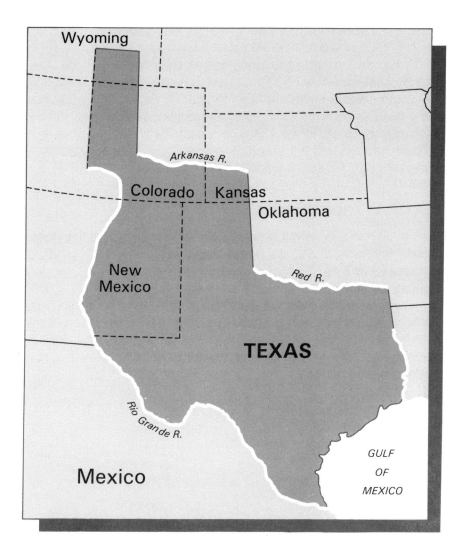

The republic of Texas consisted
of parts of Colorado, Kansas, and
Wyoming as well as New Mexico.

president worked hard at making friends with European countries. Soon France and England accepted Texas as a republic.

President Lamar urged Congress to pass two important laws. The Homestead Act of 1839 promised that no landowner would lose his farm because he was unable to pay his debts. The next year, the Education Act set aside land for two universities and land in each county for schools. Although it was many years before free schools opened and the universities were built, Mirabeau Lamar is known as the "Father of Education."

SETTLERS FROM EUROPE

During the republic, Texas grew rapidly. More people from the United States arrived and started farms and businesses. Thousands of Europeans arrived by ship from Germany, France, Austria, Ireland, Poland, and other countries.

Texas was a meeting place of peoples. No matter where they came from or why they sought to live in Texas, settlers faced common hardships. Because life in the new settlements was difficult, people were drawn together, and they became Texans—with a new pride in a new country.

TEXAS JOINS
THE UNION

Some of the people wanted Texas to remain a republic. But many more wanted Texas to join the United States. On December 29, 1845, Texas became the twenty-eighth state. It was the only state admitted to the Union that was once a separate nation.

WAR WITH MEXICO

Almost immediately after joining the United States, a dispute arose over the boundary between Texas and Mexico. To settle the quarrel, President James K. Polk offered to buy the Southwest from Mexico. When that did not work, he sent General Zachary Taylor and his army to the disputed area. On May 12, 1846, the United States declared war on Mexico.

For two years, the two nations fought from Texas to California and throughout Mexico. When American armies captured Mexico City, the war ended. The Treaty of Guadalupe Hidalgo fixed the Rio Grande as the boundary between Texas and Mexico. Also, Mexico gave up its claim to Texas and a vast section of land in the West, including the present states of New Mexico, Arizona, California, Nevada, Utah, and parts of Colorado and Wyoming. For this land, the United States paid Mexico 15 million dollars.

A spat then occurred between Texas and the United States over territories to the west of Texas. Although the United States dis-

agreed that these lands belonged to Texas, Congress settled the matter. In the Compromise of 1850, the federal government paid Texas 10 million dollars for renouncing its claims. Some of this money was used for settling debts, but Texans earmarked a large portion for growth.

THE WESTWARD MOVEMENT

As pioneers pushed the frontier westward, many small settlements developed into bustling towns. By 1860, there were more than 604,000 people in Texas; that was three times the number there had been in 1850. The largest group were Anglo-Americans (descended from white, English-speaking immigrants) from the South. Blacks made up the second largest group. But only about four hundred blacks lived free; more than 182,500 were slaves. About twenty thousand Germans composed the third largest group of settlers. Mexicans made up the next largest group. French people, Czechs, Norwegians, Swedes, and Poles also lived in Texas.

Fort Davis, now a National Historic site, was ordered to be built in 1854 by Jefferson Davis, U.S. Secretary of War, as a watering stop and protected stronghold for gold seekers.

TEXAS LEAVES
THE UNION

Many people thought slavery was wrong. They felt that no person should be allowed to own another. In the South, slaves could not marry, own property, testify in court, or win their freedom. Those opposed to slavery lived mainly in the heavily populated industrial North. Because the North had a short growing season, there were not many large farms and there were few slaves.

To destroy slavery, northern abolitionists (people who wanted to get rid of slavery) organized the Underground Railroad, which helped runaway slaves escape. Several northern states also passed personal-liberty laws, encouraging people to disobey federal laws providing for the return of fugitive slaves.

Still, slavery flourished in the South, where large plantations from Virginia to Texas raised cotton, tobacco, sugar, and other crops for profit. Some 4 million slaves made up nearly a third of the South's population in 1860. Without slave workers, many southerners claimed the agricultural South would die.

President Abraham Lincoln called the nation "a house divided ... half slave and half free." But most Texans sided with the South. Fearing President Lincoln would hinder their right to handle slavery as they pleased, Texans voted to secede from the Union on February 23, 1861.

Along with ten other southern states, Texas formed the Confederate States of America. The twenty-three states that did not secede from the Union remained part of the United States of America. Because Governor Sam Houston would not sign an oath of allegiance to the Confederacy, he was put out of office.

WAR BETWEEN THE STATES

War between the North and the South broke out on April 12, 1861, and lasted for four terrible years. The Civil War was the worst war in American history. (A civil war occurs when the people of a country disagree and try to settle the problem by fighting.)

Early in the war, the Union navy blockaded the Texas coast, captured Galveston, and gained control of the seaports. President Lincoln strengthened the North's war effort and weakened the South's when he issued the famous Emancipation Proclamation on New Year's Day 1863. It stated that all the slaves in the Confederacy were free. (Emancipation is the act of setting free. A proclamation is a public declaration.)

The last battle of the war was fought in Texas at Palmito Ranch, near the mouth of the Rio Grande, on May 13, 1865. Back then, messages traveled slowly, so soldiers were unaware that the South had lost the war thirty-five days earlier at Appomattox, Virginia.

AFTERMATH OF WAR

After the war, a group of people sympathetic to the Union's cause called the Radicals rose to power in Texas and angered many southerners. Lawlessness and racial violence against blacks erupted, as southern whites formed powerful secret societies like the Ku Klux Klan.

The federal government sent General Gordon Granger and eighteen hundred Union soldiers to oversee the rebuilding of Texas. During Reconstruction, Texas was ruled by a military government, an appointed governor, and three governors elected by the Radicals. The military government set up a new state government, which denied anyone who had fought for the Confederacy an office; it also carried out the Emancipation Proclamation. It was more than two years after the declaration before Texas slaves finally learned that they were free.

Most southerners thought themselves superior to blacks. As a result, many southern states—including Texas—passed laws called black codes that were aimed at regulating black labor and maintaining the superiority of whites. During Reconstruction, blacks could not bear arms, serve on juries, or attend schools with whites. In addition, those not working could be arrested for vagrancy and hired out to employers.

THE PROBLEMS OF RECONSTRUCTION

The first years of Reconstruction were especially difficult for Texas and the South. Since the war had been fought mainly in the South, the widespread destruction left cities and towns, plantations and farms, and railroads and roads in ruins. Thousands of southerners were left poor, homeless, and without food.

Texas suffered less war damage than most of the other Confederate states. But many of its cotton fields remained unplanted after the war because there were not enough workers or tools. Some who had worked on the farms had been killed or badly wounded. Others returned from the war with little money for rebuilding the farms. The owners looked for a way to hire farm workers without paying cash.

From 1865 to 1875, a new kind of farming called sharecropping was widespread in Texas. In exchange for a share of the crops, a house, and tools, a sharecropper farmed land. Most sharecroppers were blacks who could not find paying jobs and feared the repercussions of the black codes.

The problem was sharecroppers had to purchase everything they needed solely with their crops. But usually this left little with

The Tigua Indian Reservation is the oldest
community within the present boundaries
of Texas. It was established in 1681.

which to feed their families, and there was nothing left to sell. There was also no way to save any money, so black farmers could not better their lives by starting businesses or buying land.

In 1870 Texas was readmitted to the Union. But Reconstruction in Texas did not end until 1874, when control of the state was returned to the people. Then Texans wrote a new state constitution. The constitution of 1876 is the one under which Texans live today.

THE LAST INDIANS

Many Texans and the U.S. Army were set on ending the Indian problems. Only then, they felt, could all of Texas be settled by new peoples, and only then could the frontier be moved farther west than the center of the state.

But Texas Indians fought fiercely to hold on to their homelands. When the U.S. government tried to move the Plains Indians to reservations, or land set aside for them by the state, they fought to preserve their hunting grounds and way of life.

Repeatedly, the Texas Rangers battled Comanche and Kiowa raiding parties. Then, in the Red River War in 1874, Colonel Ranald Mackenzie defeated the Comanches, Kiowas, and Cheyennes. This defeat forced the Indians to leave their hunting grounds. Some drifted into Mexico or went to live on reservations. By the 1900s, there were only a few Indians left in Texas.

There are two Indian reservations in Texas today. The tribes living there came from other states, however.

7

THE GROWTH OF
AGRICULTURE

Slowly Texas became a leading agricultural state, raising crops and animals for profit. By 1860, about sixty thousand farmers had become valuable suppliers of food for the nation. They also supplied new textile industries with cotton and wool for making cloth. In the late 1800s, ranching—raising cattle, hogs, and sheep—became another important way of making a living. The Texas Department of Agriculture was established in 1907 to encourage the growth of farm products.

Today Texas has about 159,000 farmers, and more farms than any other state. Texas also leads the nation in beef cattle, which are raised for their meat.

COTTON, THE KING OF CROPS

Early settlers first raised cotton in the fertile river valleys of Texas and along the Gulf Coast. But Texans soon discovered that the upland soil in the northeastern part of the state was as good as the bottomlands of East Texas for raising cotton.

Farmers moved farther west into the drier parts of North and West Texas, but droughts, or long stretches of time without rain, taught them some grim lessons. They had to learn when and how to plant cotton and other crops. Using a method called dry farming, they learned to plow land so that the soil helped hold the rain.

*Farming grew slowly in Texas until the state
eventually became a leading agricultural producer.*

As a result, the cotton industry grew with such great speed that the hardy plant soon earned the name "white gold." Within a few years, cotton became—and remains—Texas's most important crop. Since 1880, more cotton has been grown in Texas than in any other state (with the exception of 1982, when California beat Texas).

Today King Cotton is grown on about twenty-four thousand Texas farms. Most of the farms are in the Rolling Plains and High Plains around Lubbock; there, irrigation supplies land with water via pipes or ditches. Machinery now makes it possible for a single farmer to do the work that twenty people did in an earlier time. The machines now plow, plant, fertilize, and harvest Texas cotton.

OTHER MONEY CROPS

Once farmers on the frontier learned about dry farming and irrigation, corn, wheat, and oats also became important money-making crops.

In 1892 the first rice mill was built in Beaumont. After irrigation was introduced in 1899, Texas became a valuable rice producer. Houston became the center of the "Rice Belt."

Rice has since dropped to the number-five crop in the state. It ranks behind cotton, sorghum (used chiefly for livestock feed), corn, and wheat. Other important crops include barley, flaxseed, hay, oats, rye, and soybeans.

VEGETABLES, FRUITS, NUTS, AND HONEY

Texas farms yield large crops of cabbage, cantaloupes, carrots, onions, potatoes, tomatoes, and watermelons. All are grown in the lower Rio Grande Valley and around Corpus Christi, Jacksonville, Laredo, San Antonio, and Tyler. The lower Rio Grande Valley is also one of the nation's top fruit belts. Among the citrus fruits shipped to northern markets are grapefruits, lemons, and oranges. Strawberries, apples, peaches, and plums are other important crops.

—61

Grain became an important crop.

In addition, Texas is a leader in pecan and peanut production. Pecan trees grow along streams and rivers throughout most of the state, except in the Great Plains and the Mountains and Basins region. East and Central Texas farmers produce highly valuable peanut crops. For honey, many Texas farmers raise bees.

THE CATTLE BUSINESS

For hundreds of years, wild cattle roamed the plains of Texas. When Texas became a Republic, all cattle not branded became public property. Texans rounded up stock, marked them with their own special brands, and built large ranches.

The cattle business spread to the Panhandle and West Texas, where some of the world's largest cattle ranches were started. One was the 1,250,000-acre (500,000-hectare) King Ranch in South Texas. Another was the 250,000-acre (100,000-hectare) Pierce Ranch on the Gulf Coast.

During the Civil War, most of the men went off to fight the Union. Once again, cattle roamed freely. By the end of the war, some six million cattle grazed on open ranges.

A Texas rancher who rounded up a herd after the war could get a good price for it. There was a large market for beef a thousand miles (1609 km) away in the North. At the time, however, transporting cattle north was far from easy. Cattle had to be herded along the great Chisholm Trail and across Indian territory to the nearest railroad town, faraway Abilene, Kansas. There the herds were sold and shipped to stockyards for slaughter.

COWBOYS

Hired men called cowboys rode with the herds. Twice a year, they rounded up all the cattle and herded them to a central place in Texas. There men from area ranches sorted out the animals, branded

*Guarding the herd. Texas has
always been associated with cattle.*

*Rich land and mild winters enable
cattle to graze year round in the state.*

new calves, separated diseased animals from the herd, and selected stock for market. Then they began the Long Drive north to market. During those tiring, dangerous months, cowboys drove as many as four thousand animals in a single herd overland to Abilene. If a herd stampeded, a cowboy had to depend on his horse for regaining control. Among his other valuable tools were his gun, his saddle, and his rope.

Many cowboy songs originated on the Long Drive. The cowboy became a symbol of the strength and vigor of the "wild West." However, the Long Drive ended in 1884. Once railroads were built across Texas, there was no longer a need to drive cattle to northern markets.

By then, however, too many cattle were grazing on the range, thousands more than the land could support. Many sheep ranchers had moved onto the plains, and their herds cropped the grass so short that the cattle could not graze the land. In 1885–86 a lengthy summer drought, followed by one of the worst winters ever, caused many ranchers to sell what was left of their cattle.

For the surviving cattle owners, ranching became big business. Breeders selected and mated the best types of cattle for producing high-grade beef. Then they mated the best of those offspring until, after several generations, pure-bred cattle had the desired qualities. Ranchers found that the Texas Longhorn, which had been brought by early Spaniards, grew more slowly and was less profitable than the white-faced Hereford. During the 1920s and 1930s, the King Ranch in Kingsville crossed Shorthorns with Brahmans from India and produced a breed that was unaffected by heat and insects. The Santa Gertrudis was the first breed of cattle developed in the United States.

Because Texas has rich grasslands and mild winters, cattle can graze the year round. This meant that Texans could raise cattle more cheaply than northern farmers. Many cattlemen made huge fortunes, and gave Texas banking a boost, too.

THE FIRST RAILROADS

The first Texas railroad ran over nine miles (14.5 km) of track between Harrisburg and Houston in 1852. By the turn of the century, trains had become the chief carriers of people, freight, and cattle.

This was largely because in 1854 the Sixteen Sections Bill granted any railroad sixteen sections of land for every mile (1.61 km) of track laid beyond twenty miles (32.2 km). This meant that a railroad company that laid a hundred miles (161 km) of track received more than a million acres (400,000 hectares) of land from the state.

The bill attracted railroads to almost all parts of Texas. However, railroad companies found that the Panhandle was not populated enough to be profitable. As a result, companies there began to offer their land at bargain prices. To attract buyers, they placed nationwide advertisements that made outlandish claims about the fertility and climate of the Panhandle.

SHEEP RANCHING

While the cattle business was growing, the sheep business grew, too. Sheep ranchers from other states settled near Waco. Those from as far away as England and Scotland moved to the San Antonio area. German sheep ranchers joined other Germans already settled in Central Texas. Almost everyone brought his own pure-bred sheep and crossed them with Spanish-Mexican sheep once they were in Texas.

The growing market for wool drew even more sheep raisers to Texas. Soon flocks grazed everywhere between San Antonio and Laredo. Today Texas raises more sheep and produces more wool than any other state. Interestingly, nearly all the mohair clipped in the United States comes from Texas goats.

THE RISE OF
INDUSTRY

During the late 1800s, many Texans turned from the growing of things to the making of things. The large-scale producing and making of things is called industry. While Texas was building an agricultural empire, it was also building an industrial empire.

Until the late 1800s, factories had often been no more than shops. In the average shop, fewer than six workers manufactured, or turned raw materials into finished goods. However, even before the Civil War, Texas factories made a variety of goods: farm tools, saddles, steam engines, beer, bread, and whiskey.

After the Civil War, new industries appeared. Some plants manufactured paint, wallpaper, iron, tin, newsprint, brooms, and fertilizers. Others made ice, lime, and mineral waters. Most important of all, however, were the industries related to agriculture.

Saddles, boots, harnesses, and other leather goods were made in factories near ranching areas, then were shipped to other states. But meat was the most valued product. Fort Worth became a beef-packing center.

Cotton farming triggered the building of textile mills for making yarn and cloth. As interest in raising sheep increased, so did the manufacture of woolen goods.

Wheat, corn, and other grains grown on North Central Texas prairies prompted the growth of grain mills.

*The rise of industry in Texas. The state
went from growing things to making things.*

LUMBER

Lumbering became more important than farming in the forested parts of East Texas about 1880, once sawmills had switched from water to steam power and railroads had spread across Texas.

The best lumber was sent to factories around the heavily populated towns, where there was a hefty market for it. Factories near Houston made carriages, wagons, carts, ships, barrels, buckets, window blinds, doors, furniture, and other wood products.

In 1900, the lumber, cottonseed, and cottonseed-oil industries led all the others in the value of their products. But before long, the discovery of vast deposits of oil and natural gas in Texas created a new industry leader.

THE OIL BOOM

For hundreds of years, it was known that there was oil, or petroleum, in Texas. Yet no less an authority than the U.S. Geological Survey had said that big oil deposits would never be found in Texas, especially not near the salt domes along the Gulf Coast. The chief geologist for the Standard Oil Company agreed.

But one Texan named Patillo Higgins believed otherwise. He had a notion that the upward pressure of the salt domes was creating faults, or fractures, in the earth that were trapping large pools of oil. He noticed that nearby creeks and springs often had oil seeps or bubbled with sulfurous gases. He had also observed slight uplifts in the earth's surface at different spots along the Texas Gulf Coast. There was one uplift about a mile in diameter and fifteen feet high near Beaumont. On the flat coastal plain, it looked like a mountain. The mound was called Spindletop.

Patillo Higgins spent his life savings, plus every dollar he could beg or borrow, trying to prove his theory. In the process, he drilled a test well at Spindletop and recovered just enough oil to convince the leaders of the Pennsylvania oil industry that the prospects were worth another try.

Boiler Avenue
April 23 1903
Edgerton

*A mass of derricks made up Spindletop, typical
of the earliest drilling operations. Horses
and carts travel down a plank road in 1903.*

At a depth of 1,160 feet (354 m), the men heard a roar deep in the earth. Then the pipe stuck. Believing that a dull bit was the problem, they pulled the entire pipe out and changed the drill bit. But they never tested the new bit. Instead, on January 10, 1901, Patillo Higgins's theory was confirmed. For the next ten days, a fountain of oil shot out of the ground in a gusher nearly 160 feet (49 m) high. Before the "runaway" well was capped, it poured 800,000 barrels of oil onto the plains and formed a huge lake of oil. No Texas well had ever produced more than 1,500 barrels in a day, but Spindletop gave between 85,000 and 100,000 barrels daily.

Spindletop was the foundation of the Gulf Oil Corporation, now a subsidiary of Chevron. Texaco was also born at Spindletop, as were small companies that eventually became part of Atlantic Richfield, Mobil, and Sun. Several Spindletop workers later banded together to form another important oil company, the Humble Oil and Refining Company, now Exxon.

Only the Battle of San Jacinto had more influence on Texas history. People went wild. Soon roads were jammed with horse-drawn wagons carrying prospectors, tools, and equipment to Texas. A forest of oil derricks sprouted up. The population of Beaumont jumped from nine thousand to fifty thousand in two years. The center of the petroleum industry shifted to Texas. By 1919, 40 million barrels of oil had been produced.

Discoveries in many other parts of the state followed. Wherever large oil deposits were found, the land price jumped from a few dollars to several thousand dollars an acre.

New people brought in oil-related industries. Texans built great refineries for purifying oil and new pipelines for carrying oil. They deepened coastal harbors to help ship their oil. Manufacturing plants produced kerosene, gasoline, lubricating oils, and others. This created jobs for thousands. At the same time, they provided funding for schools, highways, and hospitals.

No one had ever dreamed that Texas had so much oil or that it would gush from so many different parts of the state. For several years, Spindletop and other Gulf Coast fields formed the center of the Texas oil industry. Later, large fields were opened in the Panhandle, in the Pecos Valley, and in Central, East, and North Texas. Eventually, the Permian Basin in West Texas and southeastern New Mexico provided more than one-fourth of all oil produced in the nation. By 1970, oil had been found in 200 of 254 Texas counties. Today, that number is even greater. In addition, there are many offshore wells in the Gulf of Mexico.

INDUSTRIAL GROWTH

Millions of barrels of crude oil gush from the land every year, making oil Texas's most valuable mineral. The second most valuable is natural gas. Texas produces about 40 percent of all natural gas in the United States.

It is not surprising, then, that Texas's top industry is oil and gas processing, or that the petrochemical industry ranks next. Petrochemicals are chemicals made from oil or natural gas. Among the leading petrochemicals made in Texas are ethylene and toluene. Ethylene is used in welding; toluene is used in making explosives and many other chemicals. Texas oil and gas also encouraged the growth of oil-producing machinery and oil-field equipment manufacturing. Today Houston is the world's largest center for manufacturing oil-related equipment.

During the early 1900s, the demand for Texas sulfur, salt, helium, and lime also grew. Graphite, magnesium, fluorospar, granite, gypsum, and coal were needed in industry, too. Large amounts of limestone were used for making cement. Brick, pottery, and tile were made from clay. Stone was used in the building industry and in road construction.

Wood was in demand for building and wood pulp for making paper. Paper manufacturing in turn triggered growth in printing and publishing. Food processing became even more important as farmers using irrigation and improved farming methods produced larger crops. The textile industry grew with the growth of cotton and wool production. And soon Texas produced more electricity than any other state. Finally, it also became a leader among states in shrimp production.

BANKING

For his own reasons, pioneer Sam Houston did not trust banks. Neither did most Texas pioneers. Many had lost money when the Mexican government failed to redeem the currency of the Banco Nacional de Texas in gold and silver. And when wildcat banks in other states failed during the panic of 1837, they left many people holding worthless paper.

Texas outlawed organized banking in the state's first constitution. But as industry grew, private investors and financial institutions were needed to provide money for expansion. Many farmers and ranchers needed supplies and groceries before they drove their cattle north to market. Private investors' financial institutions advanced them money on credit before they sold their crops or cattle.

The era of private banking ended in 1905, when state bank charters were authorized. With the coming of oil and the subsequent industrial growth, Texas banking began to rival money center giants in the east. Ever since Texas opened its borders to interstate banking in 1987, there have been sweeping changes in the banking industry.

TRANSPORTATION

During World War I, the increasing use of cars in Texas led to the creation of the State Highway Department. More bridges and better roads were built to make traveling easier and safer. Today Texas has 250,000 miles (402,000 km) of roads and highways.

Ever since the first airline flew from Dallas to Chicago in 1927,

One of the most accessible and popular attractions at the Lyndon B. Johnson Space Center is Rocket Park, which permits close-up viewing of actual space vehicles.

Dallas has remained an important air center. Today more than thirty airlines serve Texas and its over twelve hundred airports. The largest airport is Dallas-Fort Worth.

Railroads in Texas operate over fifteen thousand miles of track, more track than in any other state. Some thirty rail lines provide freight service, while passenger trains link about twenty Texas cities.

Texas has fifteen man-made deep-water ports along the Gulf of Mexico. Houston is the busiest; it is a chief cotton-shipping center. Fifteen shallow ports also lie along the coast. They handle barges, fishing vessels, and other shallow-draft vessels.

COMMUNICATION

Today Texas publishes about 120 daily newspapers and about 500 weeklies, as well as about 465 magazines. *The Texas Almanac,* containing information about Texas, has been published since 1857.

The first Texas radio program was broadcast from Dallas on WRR in 1920. Not until 1948 was the first television program shown on WBAP-TV (now KXAS-TV) in Fort Worth. Today Texas has about 455 radio stations and about 60 television stations.

SPACE

In 1962 the National Aeronautics and Space Administration (NASA) started building a $150 million Manned Spacecraft Center in Clear Lake City, near Houston. Since 1964, it has been the headquarters and training grounds for all manned flights into space. On July 20, 1969, scientists and engineers at the center directed the Apollo 11 astronauts in their landing on the moon.

The Manned Spacecraft Center was renamed the Lyndon B. Johnson Space Center in 1973. It has made Texas a major center for space research. Several corporations design and test space equipment there. And Texas universities are doing research in space medicine.

TEXAS CITIES

A north-south line drawn from the top of Texas to the bottom, just west of Dallas, would divide the state into two different areas. In the eastern area are most of the big industrial cities. This area also has many of the cotton and rice farms, pine forests, and pecan trees. On the west side of Texas, you would find cotton, too, but it is mainly cattle, oil, and wheat country.

Large numbers of Texans choose to live in or near the cities for any of several reasons. A chief reason is that most of the manufacturing takes place around cities, so most of the jobs are there.

HOUSTON

The largest city in Texas is Houston, the energy capital of America. It has a population of more than 2 million people and is the fourth largest city in the nation.

Houston is situated on 528 square miles (1,367.5 sq km) in Harris County. Even though it lies inland—about fifty miles (80 km) from the Gulf of Mexico—it is the nation's third largest seaport. The stream known as the Buffalo Bayou, which links Houston with the Gulf of Mexico, has been widened and deepened. Only New York and New Orleans handle more cargo than Houston.

In Houston, the old world meets the new. Historical buildings of the 1800s stand in the shadows of gleaming skyscrapers. People

The ever-changing Houston skyline

wearing the latest fashions mingle with those in jeans and boots. The city offers everything from the world's largest rodeo and live-stock show to ballet and symphony concerts to country music jamborees. Restaurant fare varies from Continental cuisine to Texas chili cook-offs and chicken fried steak. There are also dense piney woods, wide open spaces, and a lot of azaleas.

On the battleground where Sam Houston led Texas to freedom is the San Jacinto Monument, the tallest monument in the world. An underground tunnel in downtown Houston links eighty-eight buildings, miles of restaurants, and bookstores and other shops.

The Houston area is the nation's top oil-refining center. Since about twenty major oil companies have headquarters in the city, it is difficult to be in town for long without hearing a lot of oil talk. The price of oil has sunk and has dragged the local economy down with it. But Houstonians still have a rosy outlook on the future. After all, oil is a commodity whose price goes up and down, just like the price of lead, silver, and zinc. For now, people are simply keeping an eye on tomorrow.

The city is strong in medical and space technology. The Texas Medical Center is respected worldwide for its advances in health care. Its eight hospitals and two medical schools attract scientists, students, and patients from all areas of the globe. Extensive research has brought international recognition in the areas of heart disease, cancer, rehabilitation, biomathematics, and aerospace medicine.

All U.S. space missions are directed from NASA's Lyndon B. Johnson Space Center in nearby Clear Lake City.

Because the Houston area is an important source of natural gas, a large percentage of the nation's petrochemicals are made here. The city is the nation's leading manufacturer of fertilizers, insecticides, and oil-field equipment. About 80 percent of the synthetic rubber produced in the United States comes from Houston, too.

There are nine colleges and universities in Houston, among them Rice University.

—79

DALLAS

Dallas is the second largest city in Texas. It is the largest banking center in the Southwest and has more insurance companies than any other city in the country. It ranks as one of the nation's major centers of communications, fashion, trade, and manufacturing, mostly of electronics and electrical equipment, aircraft, and missile parts. Dallas is also an important transportation center.

The people of Dallas often call their city "Big D." It covers about 301 square miles (780 sq km) in Dallas County in North Central Texas.

President John F. Kennedy was assassinated in Dallas on November 22, 1963. Vice-President Lyndon B. Johnson was sworn in as President aboard a presidential plane at Love Field in Dallas.

Dallas is a city of art and culture. The Dallas Civic Opera performs in the Music Hall; the New York Metropolitan Opera visits annually. The city also houses the Dallas Symphony Orchestra, the Civic Ballet Society, a metropolitan ballet, a civic chorus, and a chamber music society.

Southern Methodist University is the largest, oldest, and best-known university in the city.

SAN ANTONIO

One of the most historic cities in the United States is San Antonio. Today it is also the third largest city in Texas and a leading trade and cultural center. It is the chief market for farm products from the surrounding agricultural area. Many of its manufactured products are exported to Mexico. Much of San Antonio's cultural life reflects the city's Mexican and Spanish heritage. There are five Spanish missions in San Antonio; the Alamo is the most famous.

The city lies on rolling prairies in the Hill Country, about 150 miles (241 km) northeast of the Mexican border. Some of the nation's largest military bases are in the San Antonio area. Kelly Air Force Base is the nation's oldest military airfield.

—80

*Dallas is one of the nation's major centers
of communications, trade, and manufacturing.*

The San Antonio River surrounds downtown San Antonio. Along the riverfront are restored houses and shops in buildings built by early Spanish settlers. Visitors often ride flat-bottomed boats up and down the river.

FORT WORTH

Fort Worth is a major industrial city and one of the nation's chief aircraft producers. It is also a leading market for grain and oil. Fort Worth lies in the center of a rich oil-producing area, about thirty-five miles west of Dallas.

Major Ripley A. Arnold founded the city in 1849 as an army post to protect settlers from Indian attacks. The city's nickname, "Cow-town," derives from its history as a cattle-marketing center. After Texas and Pacific Railroad tracks reached Fort Worth in 1876, cattle were loaded into railroad cars and shipped from there rather than being driven to market in Kansas. As the cattle and grain industries grew, the city's population swelled. Fort Worth's first flour mill opened in 1882.

Six Flags Over Texas is an amusement park located near Fort Worth. The theme of the park is Texas history. Texas Christian University is in Fort Worth.

EL PASO

El Paso is on the north bank of the Rio Grande in the far western corner of Texas. It lies on the border between the United States and Mexico and is a gateway for travel between the two countries.

The fallen heroes of the Alamo are commemorated by this sculpture in San Antonio.

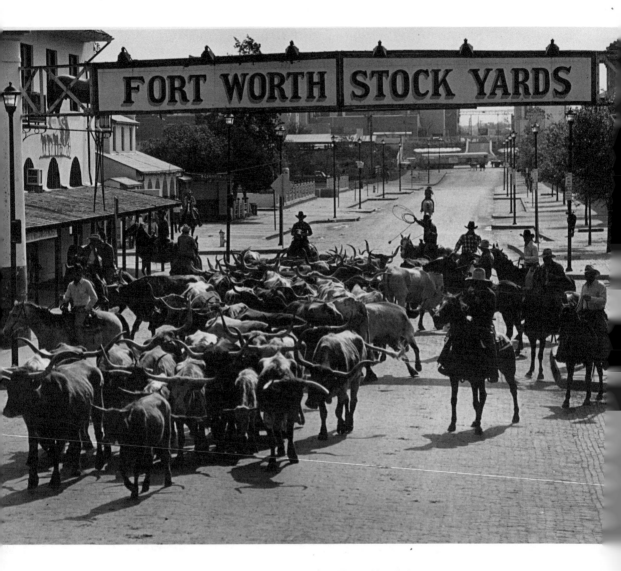

*Exchange Avenue in Fort Worth is about
the only major city street in Texas
where you can find a Longhorn cattle drive.*

*The University of Texas Tower and Main Building
are familiar landmarks in Austin.*

El Paso is an important distributing and manufacturing center. It has oil refineries, cotton mills, and stockyards.

Southeast of El Paso, the Rio Grande makes a great curve. Big Bend National Park lies inside this curve. It covers 707,895 rugged acres (283,158 hectares). The Chisos Mountains rise nearly a mile above the Rio Grande. *Chisos* is the Spanish word for ghost.

AUSTIN

Austin is the capital of Texas. It lies on the banks of the Colorado River in the central part of the state. In 1881 the state capitol in Austin was burned. A new structure made of red granite from a Texas rock quarry was dedicated in 1888 and is still in use today.

Austin is the home of the University of Texas and five other colleges. The Lyndon B. Johnson Library and Museum is also in Austin. It houses all of President Johnson's important papers from his many years of public service. One room in the library looks exactly like the Oval Office in the White House.

10

TEXAS TODAY

Texas is building a fine future on a proud past. Agriculture and mining remain important to the state's economy, but more Texans now work in manufacturing. The number of factories has more than doubled since 1945.

Many national corporations are making Texas their headquarters. Tens of thousands of people are moving to Texas from other parts of the country. They are drawn by the feeling of friendliness and the challenge of pushing forward, breaking new ground.

As Texas plans for future space trips, it also looks ahead to developing modern technologies such as computers, robots, and electronic microchips. Some Texans are working on the use of lasers in medicine, industry, and defense. And much effort is being devoted to molecular and genetic studies aimed at preventing and diagnosing diseases. At the same time, people all over Texas are working to conserve land, animals, and water for generations to come.

Everyone knows there are many wealthy Texans. Sadly, there are many, many more Texans who are poor. Texas leaders are laboring to pass laws that will improve life for all people in the state.

Texas—a state of wide open spaces and sophisticated metropolises

IMPORTANT DATES
IN TEXAS HISTORY

1519 Alonso Alvarez de Piñeda explored the coast of Texas.

1528 Alvar Nuñez Cabeza de Vaca was shipwrecked off Galveston Island.

1541 Francisco Vasquez de Coronado led an expedition across West Texas in search of gold.

1682 The first mission was built in Texas, near present-day El Paso.

1685 Robert Cavelier, Sieur de la Salle, founded Fort Saint Louis, a French settlement.

1718 The Spanish founded a mission later known as the Alamo.

1821 Texas became part of the new Empire of Mexico. Stephen F. Austin founded the first American settlements.

1830 Mexico stopped Americans from settling in Texas.

1835 The Texas Revolution began.

1836 Texas declared its independence from Mexico at Washington-on-the-Brazos.

The Alamo fell to Santa Anna's army after a thirteen-day siege.

Texans defeated Santa Anna's army at the Battle of San Jacinto and won freedom from Mexico.

Texas became an independent Republic.

Sam Houston became the first president of the Republic of Texas.

1839 The Homestead Law was enacted.

1845 Texas became the twenty-eighth state on December 29.

1846 War between Mexico and the United States began.

1848 The Texas boundary was set.

1850 In the Compromise of 1850, Texas received 10 million dollars for renouncing its claims to territories reaching far into what is now the western United States.

1852 The first railroad in Texas began operating between Harrisburg and Houston.

1861 Texas seceded from the Union.
Texas joined the Confederate States of America.

1865 The last battle of the Civil War was fought at Palmito Ranch after General Lee had surrendered at Appomattox. Word had not reached Texas.

1866 The great cattle drives from Texas began and continued for more than twenty years.

1870 Texas was readmitted to the Union.

1876 The present state constitution was adopted.

1881 The Southern Pacific Railroad linked Texas and California.

1888 The state capitol at Austin was dedicated.

1900 A powerful hurricane destroyed Galveston, killing at least six thousand people.

1901   Oil was discovered at Spindletop.

1915   Another powerful hurricane ripped Galveston, claiming 275 lives, but a new seawall saved the city from destruction.

1963   President John F. Kennedy was assassinated in Dallas.

Lyndon B. Johnson of Texas was sworn in as the thirty-sixth President at Love Field in Dallas.

1964   The National Aeronautics and Space Administration opened its Manned Spacecraft Center near Houston.

1973   The Manned Spacecraft Center was renamed the Lyndon B. Johnson Space Center.

1983   Hurricane Alicia, the most costly hurricane in history, struck the Texas coast.

1986   Texas celebrated the 150th anniversary of independence from Mexico.

FOR FURTHER READING

Bishop, Curtis, Grace Bishop, and Clyde Inez Martin. *Trails to Texas.* Austin: W.S. Benson & Co., 1965.

Callihan, Dr. D. Jeanne. *Our Mexican Ancestors.* San Antonio: The University of Texas Institute of Texan Cultures, 1981.

Flynn, Jean. *Remember Goliad.* Austin: Eakin Press, 1984.

Freedman, Russell. *Cowboys of the Wild West.* Boston: Houghton Mifflin Co., 1985.

Harmon, Jack. *Texas Missions and Landmarks.* San Antonio: The University of Texas Institute of Texan Cultures, 1978.

Moss, Helen. *Life in a Log Cabin on the Texas Frontier.* Austin: Eakin Press, 1982.

Peacock, Howard. *The Big Thicket of Texas.* Boston: Little, Brown & Co., 1984.

Richards, Norman. *The Story of the Alamo.* Chicago: Children's Press, 1970.

INDEX

Aerospace industry, 76
Agriculture
    cattle business, 63
    cotton, 59–61
    fruit, 61–63
    nuts, 63
    rice, 61
    vegetables, 61–63
Alamo, Battle of, 41–44
Atakapan Indians, 25
Austin, 86
Austin, Moses, 34–35
Austin, Stephen Fuller, 37–41

Banking industry, 74
Bowie, Jim, 44

Caddo Indians, 23–25
Cattle business, 63
Cities
    Austin, 86
    Dallas, 80
    El Paso, 83–86

Fort Worth, 83
Houston, 77–79
San Antonio, 80–83
    founding of, 32–36
Climate, 22
Coahuiltecan Indians, 25–26
Coastal Plains, 11–14
Comanche Indians, 26–27
Communication industry, 76
Constitution, Texas, 44
Coronado, Francisco Vasquez
    de, 31
Cowboys, 63–66
Crockett, Davy, 44

Dallas, 80

El Paso, 83–86

Fort Worth, 83
French explorers, 32

Great Plains, 14

Guadalupe Mountain, 16

High Plains, 14
Houston, 77–79
Houston, General Samuel, 41–47

Ibarvo, Gil, 34
Independence, Texas, 48–50
Indians
    Atakapan Indians, 25
    Caddo Indians, 23–25
    Coahuiltecan Indians, 25–26
    Comanche Indians, 26–27
    Jumano Indians, 24–25
    Karankawa Indians, 25
    Kiowa Indians, 26–27
    Lipan Apache Indians, 26–27
    ousting of tribes, 58
    Tonkawa Indians, 25–26
    Wichita Indians, 23–25
Industry
    aerospace industry, 76
    banking industry, 74
    communication industry, 76
    industrial growth, 73–74
    lumber industry, 70
    oil industry, 70–73
    transportation industry, 74–76

Jumano Indians, 24–25

Karankawa Indians, 25
Kiowa Indians, 26–27

Lakes, 16
Lamar, Mirabeau, 48–50
Lipan Apache Indians, 26–27
Lumber industry, 70

Mountains and Basins region, 16

National Wildflower Research Center, 19
Natural resources, 16–19
    climate, 22
    plants, 19
    wildlife, 19–20
North Central Plains, 14

Oil industry, 70–73

Pineda, Alonso Alvarez de, 28
Plants, 19

Railroads, 67
Reconstruction, 56–58
Revolution, Texas, 41–44
Rio Grande, 16
Rivers, 16
Runaway Scrape, 44–45

Saint Denis, Louis, 32

San Antonio, 80–83
    founding of, 32–36
San Antonio de Valero
    mission, 34
San Jacinto, Battle of, 45–47
Santa Anna, General Antonio
    Lopez de, 41–47
Sheep ranching, 67
Sieur de la Salle, Robert Cave-
    lier, 32
Spain
    Spanish explorers, 28–32
    uprising against, 36
Spanish explorers, 28–32
Streams, 16

Terrain, 11–16
    Coastal Plains, 11–14
    Great Plains, 14
    lakes, 16
    Mountains and Basins re-
      gion, 16
    North Central Plains, 14
    rivers, 16
    streams, 16
Texas
    cities, 77–86
    history of, 28–47, 89–91
    Civil War, 55
    first American colony in,
      37
    first American settle-
      ments, 36–37

French explorers, 32
immigrants to, 50
ousting of Indian tribes,
    58
pioneers, 37–40
Reconstruction, 56–58
San Jacinto, Battle of,
    45–47
Spanish explorers, 28–
    32
Texas Constitution, 44
Texas independence,
    48–50
Texas revolution, 41–44
uprising against Spain,
    36
war with Mexico, 51–53
westward movement, 53
secession from Union, 54–
    55
size of, 9
terrain, 11–16
Texas Panhandle, 14
Tonkawa Indians, 25–26
Transportation industry, 74–76
Travis, Colonel William, 41–44

Vaca, Alvar Nunez Cabeza de,
    28

Westward movement, 53
Wichita Indians, 23–25
Wildlife, 19–20

ABOUT THE AUTHORS

Betty Lou Phillips attended Syracuse University in New York, after which she taught in the Shaker Heights, Ohio, public schools. She has written for *The Cleveland Press* and *PRO Quarterback*. She is the author of nine books and is listed in the first edition of *Notable Women of Texas,* Marquis's *Who's Who Among American Women,* and Marquis's *Who's Who in the World.* Today she lives with her husband, John Roach, and her three sons in Houston, Texas.

Bryce Phillips is a student at Texas Christian University in Fort Worth. During the summer months, a love of nature lures him to his farm in Sequin, sixty miles east of San Antonio. *Texas* is Mr. Phillips's first book.